Muffled Cries

Dr. Gregory Elayadom

BLUEROSE PUBLISHERS
India | U.K.

Copyright ©Dr Gregory Elayadom 2023

All rights reserved by author. No part of this publication may be reproduced, stored in a retrieval system or transmitted in any form or by any means, electronic, mechanical, photocopying, recording or otherwise, without the prior permission of the author. Although every precaution has been taken to verify the accuracy of the information contained herein, the publisher assume no responsibility for any errors or omissions. No liability is assumed for damages that may result from the use of information contained within.

BlueRose Publishers takes no responsibility for any damages, losses, or liabilities that may arise from the use or misuse of the information, products, or services provided in this publication.

For permissions requests or inquiries regarding this publication, please contact:

BLUEROSE PUBLISHERS
www.BlueRoseONE.com
info@bluerosepublishers.com
+91 8882 898 898
+4407342408967

ISBN: 978-93-5741-773-0

Printed in INDIA

Cover design: [Muskan Sachdeva]
Typesetting: [Pooja Sharma]

First Edition: June 2023

Dedicated with gratitude to:

Rt. Rev. Dr. Vijay Anand, Bishop Emeritus, Diocese of Chanda for the wonderful and challenging opportunities given and to the many Priests who stood by me through thick and thin.

Acknowledgement

This flight would not have been possible without the Almighty who loves and stands by me and enlightens my understanding and strengthens my faith in humankind.

With grateful heart I say a big thank you to Prof.(Dr.) G. K. Ghanshyam, who was kind enough to write a Foreword to this Anthology of poems. Dr.Ghanshaym, **Professor of English, Directorate of Higher Education, Nava Raipur, Atal Nagar, Chhattisgarh,** is a renowned educationist, a prolific writer and an eloquent speaker.

My parents who taught me to connect with the heart as well as the mind and to craft some kind of meaning to the human struggle.

My wife Chanda and sons Bruno and Bonie and their families who provide me with a pleasing atmosphere wherein I find a serene and exhilarating, mysterious and inviting feel like the forests and streams of Wayanad; though they fondly complain that I write only about "the sad music of humanity."

My friend Dr. T.K. Titus who continually encourages me to fly higher and higher. But my God knows that I can neither sing like the soulful song of a Nightingale or soar high like the Skylark.

My students who suffused with a glow of warmth taught me the joy of dealing with individual souls and let me acknowledge that I always got a kind of inexplicable joy moving in and out of every lecture hall.

Credit for the cover photograph goes to my friend Rev.Fr.Tomy Chittinapilly, a humble pastor at St. Joseph Syro Malabar Catholic Church, Hamilton and St.Mother Teresa, Syro Malabar Catholic Church, Niagara Falls, Canada.

Bluerose Publishers and their wonderful team for their conscientious and diligent work which made this Anthology to see the light of the day.

Foreword

"The moving finger writes; and, having writ, moves on: nor all thy piety nor wit shall lure it back to cancel half a line, nor all thy tears wash out a word of it.- Omar Khayyam

The beauty of life is not subject to things high and mighty but to trivial things that we usually overlook in our hurry to live a life devoid of truth, of beauty, of wonder and of ecstasy. Life is an expression of love, a joy experienced in the innocent smile of a child with wistful eyes, a beauty flower blossoming in the dirty trench, the first rays of sunlight breaking through the thick of clouds or a moonlight full of romantic apprehensions. Beauty too lies in pain, in the tears melting our heart down, our eyes like the soft murmuring of a mountain stream or the torrents of a raging wild storm making our heart beat faster.

Poetry is quite vibrant and expansive. It is a virtual 'Pushpak' accommodating all with enough space in a melodious garden with the fragrance of many hues. Imagination and inspiration enables a poet to span earth and heaven, scan the fathomless deep and garner shimmering dew drops, cheerful pearls and winsome whispers of the soul.

Dr. Gregory Elayadom's Anhology of Poems 'Muffled Cries' is an attempt to write the pure poetry which touches and elevates the soul to feel the real essence of Mother

Earth, nature, human cries and relationships.

Dr. Gregory doesn't subscribe to any *ism*. He stays apart with his own style by depicting the tragedies of life, longing for hometown, broken relationships, plight of the educated unemployed, the purity of nature, changing times and various other aspects of human life.

Hailing from a village, Payyampally in Wayanad district of Kerala surrounded by mountains, forests, rivers and the aboriginals, Dr. Gregory puts forth his heart in the form of poems with remarkable clarity of thoughts and transparent expressions. Starting from the poem ' "Weird Dream" ' to the last "Shadows and Ripples" Dr. Gregory's expressions are frank and conversational in style which lends elegance to this banquet of poems

Dr. Gregory, a keen observer paints the prevailing situations brilliantly

The tragedy of people waiting for someone else to rescue them never realising that they themselves should achieve the sanity and harmony in their interpersonal relationships (Uprooted)

The poet expresses his longing for his hometown in a melodious tone.

A sad longing for that time we never grasped and wondering whether my rumbling reach out to the realms of the spirit and animal from speech to silence of seasons changing;

(Rumbling)

Nature lures Dr. Gregory's mind and heart to a greater extent by engulfing him deep into the eternal beauty of Mother Earth.

A full moon beamed its benevolence on her face totally mesmerizing in its sensuous charm and grace. (With Nature)

Notice how the poet introduces the temperaments of the modern world;

The advent of spring fails to warm up the air feeling of fear and flight, the travails of life (Dreams)

He also dwells at length on the contemporary issues related to climate change and sustainable development.; though Nature continually teaches the world that "climate change is as real as price rise". (Lost Chance)

This volume of poetry impresses the reader with its underlying rhythm, love of freedom expressed in a gay abandon and philosophical ideas delicately lacing the poems. Being an ardent admirer of nature, a teacher of literature, and a native of God's own country has exquisitely narrated the ecosystem and facets of human life.

I hope more anthologies of beautiful poems would see the light of the day from the moving fingers of Dr. Gregory Elayadom.

Dr. G. A. Ghanshyam

Professor of English

Directorate of Higher Education

Nava Raipur, Atal Nagar

Chhattisgarh

Contents

An Anthology of Poems

Weird Dream 2

Eluding Resolution 4

Longing 6

Uncertainty.. 7

Fleeting Joy 9

Summer Rains 10

Dilemma... 12

Questions 14

Stillness.. 16

Determination 18

Lost Glory 20

Paradox 22

Uprooted 24

Rumbling 25

Enchantment 27

Death 29

Love 31

With Nature 33

Educated Unemployed	35
A Day Out	37
Stupor	39
Brooding	41
A Leap into the Void	43
Pervading Power	45
One with Nature	47
Flicker of Hope	49
Wayanadan Farmers	51
Unreal Melody	53
Churning	55
Unsettled Mind	57
Nostalgia	59
Crisis of Conscience	61
Conflict Zone	63
Riverside Village	65
Election Fever	68
Mind	70
Existential Crisis	72
Change	74
Dalits	76
Baffling	78
Dreams	80

End	82
Peace and Tranquility	84
A Conceptual Crisis	86
Lost Chance	88
A Leap into the Void	90
Death	92
Refuge	94
Shadows and Ripples	96

An Anthology of Poems

Weird Dream

I see life killing so many daily
the ungainly sadness of creatures
pushing and struggling to live.
Searching for the breathing living people
but seeing only the human struggle to craft
some kind of meaning, some idea of beauty,
from the brutal inevitability of death.
Hoped Nature could save us by lifting
us above ourselves from this life
which is like a tragic love story.
This brooding meditation on loss, addiction,
this uselessness of being true to one's self
when that self itself is sadly flawed…
Yet the complicated and complex lives
defining my experience though emotionally
engaging- this spectacle of life
in this shrinking space for disagreement,
from this inwrought fairy-tale sense of doom
beyond the reach of my comprehension
like some weird and extremely vivid dreams,

the very unpredictable nature of life and death-
the two inseparable forces in nature so profound
and a non-perceptive world trying to decipher the
paradox.

Eluding Resolution

Reflecting on the brevity and breath of time
and life, romance, history and adventure
war's horrors, love's joys and obsession's peril
and identity's complexities with the realisation
that resolution can evade and frustrate;
yet life is a story of survival, a battle against
fate or a long struggle for enchanting love;
a love that transcends time and distance
a life that connects the past and present-
love the most unique thing in all history
and my life, crisp and daunting with the peaks
of mountains in an isolated village in Wayanad.
A lovely meditation on how men and women
meet the world's harsh demands and how
they wrestle with their humanity in the process
of life at once violent and lovely, hopeful and despairing?
Want to reach that place of awakening
of mind and soul that is sure to settle deeply
on to the immeasurable heaven's dome
above and beyond while one experiences

the miracle of ravishing imagery
and startling revelations
and the air of gloom and anxiety evaporate
and sweet music floating in from a different universe.

Longing

Locked up in that little world of mine
with a hopeless sense of isolation
trying to unravel the jumbled threads
of a crumbling life of an imperfect
person living in an imperfect world
watching the countless shapes of people
walking through this inherently unfair world
and trying to smash the illusory castle I built .
Afternoon deepened and twilight approached
and dark clouds gathered low and heavy
and the rains started pouring without any wind;
hurrying to my swamp through an oppressive
atmosphere.
No flapping of wings heard in the woods
only the rains did pour into the murky
depths of my consciousness growing numb.
I long for a world filled with peace and laughter
and experience the pure transparent beauty
and the lingering reverberation of a soulful song
leading to the windows of a world beyond
and sleep deeply shrouded in the darkness
of that curious little mysterious silent world.

Uncertainty

The parched earth is drenched by the rains
lending everything a glorious air
of a Wayanadan landscape so fair.
The hills wearing a deep brilliant green
the faint chill of the wind and hills
the pool of a limpid spring singing
spinning into existence inside my mind
the late summer light filtering through the branches
bringing alive a variety of dreams and goals
life offers like the fragrance of a new season.
Yet a dark limbo somewhere inside me
where all the important memories heaped
slowly turning into mud reminds
that in the midst of life everything
revolves around death the inevitable end.
A strange, lonely, helpless sort of feeling
when struggling to see into my own heart
like the interior of a house dark and gloomy
where the shadow of death slowly eats away
at the region of life and before you know

the world is full of problems far more
urgent and relevant than Greek Tragedies
the scene feel unreal and strangely distant
the brief spell of the late summer afternoon vanished.

Fleeting Joy

The weight of things unknown and unsaid
a world vast and lost and unknowable
and my dreams; a spark bobbling on a dark sea;
with a mood turning bleaker and darker
all childhood dreams and associations vanishing,
even the echo of my own footsteps frightening
like some fatal inborn defect incurable ;
a life stretching out bleakly, lonely and pathetic
all the time moving forward into darkness
like human endeavour from the dawn of time;
vast impersonal streams of people wandering
all in the pain of growing old and looking
for a glow of warmth that nourishes a peaceful light
a radiance that glows on the face of a child.
I look for a breath of fresh air that nourishes
images that strike the heart and set it
blooming like a flower in the wilderness ;
beauty that you can spend your whole life
looking for, and never find like Tantalus
dying of thirst while in very sight of relief.

Summer Rains

Scattered drops of rain begin to tap on the roof
the blinding lightenings and deafening thunder
and the biting wind flowing into my face.
The valley road hugged the river silently flowing
forest of deciduous trees lined the sides
and flapping of wings echoed from the woods.
Suddenly it started pouring; rain and more rain
and the wind moaning in my ears.
The mind wandering from one memory to another
some sad, some pleasant; and above the ridge
floated a border of pale sun light.
Another layer of clouds has darkened
and the rains started pouring again
and the shapes of the river kept changing like ripples
spreading over the calm surface of deep waters
and the wind swept the low hanging clouds.
These sights no longer invigorate or animate me
as the world is much stranger than we think or feel
and at times the wrong way is the right way.
Is death a kind of magnificent detachment

not as the opposite but as a part of life?
A frightened sense of constraint envelopes me
I wish to be in a land where time does not exist.

Dilemma

A life full of possibilities and expectations
and a complicated sadness on the face of youth;
a seemingly unbreakable silence between
them and their near and dear ones confusing;
all aiming at unachievable goals so rosy
leading to lifelong regrets and quiet despair:
life's funny way of intervening.
Youth trying to flee multiple hardships
and multi-layered complexities of life
and the fear of failing the aspirations of parents
falling a prey to drugs, sex and violence
and a life of sadness and depression.
Hoping to reach that place of awakening
of mind and soul that is sure to settle deeply
to the immeasurable heaven's dome
above and beyond where one experiences ecstasy;
but experiencing only a smile so hollow
and a glaring sense of unreality so frightening
like a dream and waking up moment
between dream and day light where everything merges

leading to a wall of disjointed sensations
In this profound sinking like an expanse of memory opened up
with snapped threads, fragments lost and untraceable
that leave them gasping and feel that the world
has ever been anything but dead for them;
and grief and despair pounding over them in waves
and life a dream where the details get fainter
the harder they try to grasp the depth and distance.

Questions

Trying to grapple with life with equanimity
in some reality striving the ideal.
The only truth that matters to me
Is the ones that I don't or can't understand.
With light headedness and a fatigue rare
I feel drastically out off from myself
and submerged memories from childhood
reflections danced and shimmered in the mind.
The lovelier stretch of road straight and desolate
through the thick dark forest and the moon
riding high above the clouds unconcerned
while I search for a kind of Vedic serenity.
Never rapt and consumed by the Sublime
constantly asking am I influenced
by the unfortunate alignment of stars?
There was a time when I was lured by
visionary frenzy; but now only cloudbursts of memories.
Blackness closing over my head when the echo
Why worry "look at the lilies of the field"
and I fondly ask "do I smell like a funeral wreath ?"

Beautiful objects connecting me to larger beauty
make me ask what is worth living for
and what is worth dying for
and what is completely foolish to pursue?
Do I have a home in some exotic place
or am I looking for something I shall never find
or is it simply "a tale told by an idiot ?"

Stillness

At times my mind forlorn and chilled
like falling back into a bewildering old dream;
a dream like mangle of past and present
a miraculously intact childhood world
where the present contained bright shard
of the living past damaged and eroded
but not destroyed or like a lense magnifying
a world transfigured in relation to the past.
The world we live in and it's uncertainty
extremely depressing with no life affirming stuff.
Yet Nature beckons like a loving mother
and time spent with her is never a waste
but like bone fire sparks flying in the darkness
she lightens my path in the darkest moments
and endows me with an internal sweetness
inexplicable to a world lost in bewilderment.
Her hug so strong and parental, at times fierce
her hand so heavy like an iron anchor;
but when crushed and oppressed by the unknowable,
her mysterious presence like a soothing balm on wounds.

At times her chilling gaze dispels unwelcome emotions
giving a sense of a stillness so profound;
a sense of huddled anonymity so pleasing;
a pure bliss and perfect heaven on earth
and I loose myself in that unnatural stillness
like spring deepening into summer in all its glory

Determination

The air is filled with the chirping of birds
and some pigeons on the window ledge;
trying to recall all the best memories of childhood
longing to go back and change what had happened .
The bright and tender sun rays invite me
to unfurl my wings and sail away over the hills
taking in all the beauty and bloom of the mountains
and walk through the winding paths along the
jungle trails
experiencing the calm pulsating nature's touch
giving a feeling of drifting between dreaming and
sleeping
and the silence of an alternate universe
enveloping my being and all memories fading
to a moth like flicker and an eerie silence ,
and all the surging billows of doubts and fears vanish
into a growing consciousness of duty before right;
walking back with a mind filled with determination
to face an unequal world badly out of joint.
The sky darkened rapidly, darker every second

the wind rustled the trees the new leaves
stood out tender against black clouds
and the rain slapped hard in the face
while the deafening wail of clouds dashing
against each other,
shivering, breaths rasping and uneven,
onward I walked, walked into it
with renewed vigour and unfaltering steps.

Lost Glory

"God's own Country" my beloved State
truly called "A Bedlam" by the Great Sage ;
where in the past thrived a society based on values
with a wonderful heritage of Mahabali
who sacrificed his kingdom to keep his word .
A society where justice and equality prevailed
and crimes never heard of, and people contended
and a river of compassion flowing through the minds
connecting everyone with loving caring and sharing.
But today the society no more at peace;
with rulers who came to power to set everything right
becoming millionaires through unlawful means
and the common man pressed down
by the weight of ever growing cost of living
crying for justice, change and rule of law.
Every dissenting voice brutally suppressed
where bribery in cash and kind, the order of the day,
where people are forced to suffer in silence
and mob psychology destroys public property
and I can see the depth of the seven seas

in the trickling drops of hapless victims.
Forced to live in a profit driven society
where even a starving tribal mercilessly killed
for stealing bread to quieten his crying stomach ?
and his pain the reason for others' smile ;
people are sick of this stinking hatred filled society
degenerating into a ritualistic one
and long for peace and tranquility igniting
the power of love, not hatred and wish
that love the magic that transforms
all things into power and beauty.

Paradox

There are worlds within each of us
that make the richest man and woman
seem tragically worthless fools and paupers ;
mind the mysterious home of paradoxes.
What makes me most normal is knowing I am not normal.
In an intimate atmosphere of love and care
we have to build our world one brick at a time ;
we believe whatever we want to believe,
but with precise language we can stir emotions ;
it is not a drive through scenic places in fancy cars.
For many in this world what is left is pain and suffering.
There are times when I stare at the grains
of light suspended in that silent space
and think of going back to the wilderness
as I am tired of this insanely bureaucratic system.
The great tragedy of the world is we cannot choose
what we want and don't want: the curse of humankind.
Am I the only one who is not truly
part of this scene and feel lonely and forlorn?
Things go on occurring and recurring

and God remain anonymous as usual
and I am desperate to hide the shameful
threadbare self that I am; always struggling
continually to escape from myself
while desperately clinging to myself
and will to care with no reason and love with no expectation.

But I can never be the great Noah, the great
conservator ; the great caretaker of the old ;
or provide a rapturous escape from the great deluge.

Uprooted

The tragedy of people uprooted from the land
that held the memories of their people and hope;
driven out by political upheaval, persecution,
civil war, natural calamities and bulldozer justice.
You find them in refugee camps or in the vast
slums of alien or native lands, and others
in self imposed internal exile bleak;
others stranded among strangers in their own land.
These alarms that alert the outside world
to understand and respond creatively
to developmental trust and skills for self help
acknowledging the mental and emotional costs
of this perhaps avoidable disaster.
The tragedy of people waiting for someone else
to rescue them never realising that they
themselves should achieve the sanity
and harmony in their interpersonal relationships
and solve the tension and strife in all relationships
learning to act together for the healing of the world
realising that we are all branches of the same tree
and part of a vast web of brothers and sisters
determined to help restore the health of our world.

Rumbling

I have been far away for too long
from the lush and rich biodiversity
of Wayanad, a place to be experienced
where a continuous soft twilight
punctuated by silent aurora dances
in the hollow blue cloudless skies.
In days bygone everything was as we dream it,
larger than life with the rainy days
the slanting thatched roofs safer than the concrete ones
where the tale of rainy season never ends
and a young adulthood humanity always on the move.
I seek to understand their own visions
of their history and look for anyone
who looks like they might remember
the stories of a lucid past where
the impossible may once have happened;
and understand the power of human language
they used to speak with the world
rather than to define it away into silence.
A sad longing for that time we never grasped

and wondering whether my rumbling reach out
to the realms of the spirit and animal
from speech to silence of seasons changing;
to open my own mind to horizons new and world outside
where my life would float like hidden blocks
of ice in the dark swirling sea of confusion
suppressing parts of my life that rise
above the surface into the sky of my memories.
Yet I have to return to the crime and crowds;
darkness and light make no sense without each other

Enchantment

In this soaring temperature and growing hatred
love to see the land shaping my eyes and eyes
cut the land and the self regulating planet into "scapes".
The landscape changes: autumn to winter,
winter to spring suffering it's own terminal diseases;
that nothing is unseasonal no death unnatural;
nothing escapes…
I see the blend of beauty; the emptiness of a bubble
that ultimately must explode into thin air
and see what is, rather what aught to be.
Yet the interdisciplinary feast of thought
the human desire to know ourselves in essence
and heal the unsettling profile of a troubled world,
where the seeds of inspiration, of hope of alarm
and of reckoning and seeking recreation,
relaxation and solitude to listen to discover
life under the shelter of the luminous heavens
and realise the world is like an ocean of petrified waves
where twilight still lingers up here on the mountains.
You need only to listen to discover life,

there is no sweeter music than the sound
of shallow water flowing over the pebbles of the jungle stream.
In a minute or two the twilight will fade completely
and I shall be left alone here in the dark.
My heart is pounding in my throat
and long for the comforts of home and hearth.
I peer into darkness but see nothing and listen
but no sound comes; all is quiet in the Wayanadan forest;
I long for the dawn it's soft glow
to discover the blue curve of eternity
and care with no reason and love with no expectation.
I cherish the luxury of this relative solitude;
still unbroken from the shimmering vantage of the living
wondering whether there is a clean timeless place
that vaults on either side of this one and breathe
as hard as I can till my last breath mingles
with the Soul of Nature pulsating eternally.

Death

Memories flooded me
like an ever-rolling stream
as I stood beside him
who lost his mother.
Death the inevitable
like love uncompromising
seizes upon humankind
with irresistible force.
Death's proximity helped me
as it struck by a far deeper
appreciation of being part
of a loving community
of deeply cherished friends
and relationships.
Tears at the passing of a dear one
are the greatest tribute
for the deep, deep mystery
of life and death.
They express a sense of pride
of honour of having known

the person who left behind
a legacy of life well lived.
We do not face
life and death alone
as we are born into a web
of relationships.

Love

Love and mutual understanding in every smile
respect and admiration in an atmosphere of happy sharing
radiating pleasure and excitement unlocking
the secrets of the soul
and a blush creeping into her cheeks as her mind
becomes alight with vivid images my face conjures up.
Grey eyes sending sparks of recollected mirth
like sunlight streaming in through a crack in the curtain.
She is that volatile mixture of child-woman
poised on the brink of adolescence with confused eyes
as I gaze into the flickering of her tender flames,
her glittering eyes and flaming cheeks like the first light of the day,
living in a climate of trust and friendliness so pure
like a silvery moon suspended like a giant football
outside the window illuminating the pale oval of her face,
causing little ripples of pleasure from her responding body

-

love the finest foundation for trust which unite two individuals.
The sun had dipped behind the trees and temperature dropped as cold wave shrouded my body
only to relax into the welcome warmth of her comforting body.
The moon made a brief appearance from behind
the clouds and for a moment everything blazed
like a match struck in the darkness thick.
Waking up to find the woman you loved smiling
at you is the very best way to begin a day
or keeping the cheeks against the soft pillow
until the birds rouse with their dawn clamours
knowing that she is there to care and share.
But when she is away there is a numbing loneliness…
and long nights filled with restlessness begin.
The evening of life draws near and tired smiles
on faces we look out through the window
and catch glimpses of light on the river
and a crazy, giddy wave of sensation
sweep us to a wild culmination of love pure
gazing at in a sort of wonder, all pains dissipate
and for a long heart stopping moment
our eyes seem to devour each other
and wish to slip into eternity gazing at each other.

With Nature

My mind a jumbled mess of needs and desires
when I saw Nature relaxed into a luxurious comfort of her home
with a smile that tingled right down her toes
and breathing in the balmy air of the tropics
to share the breathtaking sight of the land from the air
to watch the barrier reef on to which the waves
crushed and spurted white foam of glorious bubbles
while the deep green of the vegetation looking
lushly tropical as did the dancing masses of palm trees
crowding the coast line; a moment of beauty
nature had created and adorned with unique and loving care.
This magical place creates layers of translucence
that would engrave in my memory for eternity.
The softness of the water lapping my body
brought to mind the bold and bright, beautiful
and intelligent, vivacious and infinitely
attractive person beside me to behold,
and the question that niggled at my mind all day

was that never had I seen anyone so intriguingly beautiful;
someone romantic and realist at the same time.
A full moon beamed its benevolence on her face
totally mesmerizing in its sensuous charm and grace.
Ecstatic to spend all the hours of the day in
blissful forgetfulness
with nature, with a special sense of togetherness
floating under the stars reveling in a sense
of total freedom with each other like the mingling
of bodies and souls in a harmonious rhythm of life.
Enjoying the lulling swell and ebb of the waves
keeping my body light and buoyant and youthful
and mind reminding there was no point
in worrying about the sad music of humanity';
but my heart defying all acts of will
and persisting in twisting itself into uncertain life knots.
I try to leave other people's problems behind
and immerse myself in sharing the pleasures of the beauty
around me with a contended look on my face.

Educated Unemployed

The injustice of unemployment rang through his voice
the nasty premonition fast becoming unpleasurable reality
the tale of woe from unsuccessful applicants
using language effectively with care, consciousness and simplicity
and no eyes glowing with brilliant satisfaction
only fighting an abject wave of despair.
The routine factual walk into the interviewers
who would inevitably brighten or darken future,
he longed for an ecstasy of relief and delight;
a reluctant spark of expectation glistening eyes;
and an effervescent madness seized him
as he discovered only super humans unsympathetic ;
and he fumbled some words with machine gun rapidly
and a telltale response to the primitive blaze
of desire had unwittingly provoked in his mind.
Taking coffee in a silence that twanged
and mouth thinning into a grimly constrained line
and images of sharing a paradise with parents
flashed across his mind with the fascinating landscapes.

The callous lack of consideration in authorities
and rejected and dejected yet with defined dignity
of a king scorning unworthy criticism
he crossed the room into the open air.
The voices wobbling with the weight of a thousand
disappointed hopes, the elevator at the top floor
zoomed him down to the world of the unemployed;
and the flood of tears that kept him chocking -
the unemployed are free to weep any time.
"There is none so blind as those who don't want to see."
The snarling educational loans, growing inequality
the unbearable sadness and sighs of parents
and silence stretching endlessly between them
and the crazy giddy waves of sensation sweeping him
to a wild culmination of dejection
before the collective aspirations so pervading.
And in a massive exercise in futility in the face of sinking earth
forcing to leave his own land for opportunities
in countries far and alien, away from "God's own Country."

A Day Out

As the clouds of depression creep over me
I take the forest trail, trees forming green walls on either side
the deep heavy fog of lethargy washing over me
I long for the solace in the forests of Wayanad
to capture the magic of Mother Nature and experience
the indefinable-life-changing moments to live
the life of my dreams in an invisible realm.
A wordless communication passing between us
like a note hovering poignantly in the silence
in the empty shadowed meadow of the forest
with a craggy peak in the distance
where the silence lengthening in the lonely place.
I can hear the river close by in the hidden
obscurity of the forest like a mysterious being.
She flows across the untouched forest with
a movement so graceful with an endearness so natural.
At times the trumpeting of wild tusker echoes
in the forest and panic bubbling in my chest
and the flurry of deers lasting a few seconds

and hearing sounds of passage much too faint.
A disturbing and sinister look in the eyes of tigers
making me terrified into absolute immobility
then the Mother draws me into the protecting
enclosure of her hands and wiping the tears
streaking noiselessly down my face with a smile.
The silent moment flies away and my
Imagination knows no limit and the hazy
thoughts and dreams melt into the grey light
streaking across a cloudless sky as the sun
fall behind making the atmosphere surreal
enabling me to live the life of dreams so refreshing.
As the evening closed over me, homeward I turn
and a few streaks of sunlight escaped to the west,
and all the confusion and sorrow dulled
by a sleepiness seeping through my weary limbs.

Stupor

In the twilight of my life, gazing at sunset
humane and compassionate, I rest
under the protecting shadow of trees
in the eloquent silence of nature
I hear Mother Nature humming a melody
sounding like a lullaby, I didn't recognise.
The bubbling music of a stream close by
like the gentle cadence of an earlier generation
trying to conquer the boundaries of a destiny.
I see a generation whose streams of gratitude
and generosity withering in all dimension of life
not realising what is not given is lost;
the celebration of life by caring and sharing;
not finding the rays of love and joy
to accept the reality than to transcend.
I am full of ancient grief and a tingle of fear;
may be thinking things insane loosing
the trail of thought in a trans like state;
a heavy stupor clouding my mind,
logic or common sense not on my side

trying to gather my jumbled thoughts
the overpowering craving to find solution
for all the misery and suffering of the world
helpless I wish a peaceful dreamless life
for the exploited, marginalised and forsaken.
Yet the never ending streams of questions
and trying to ignore irrational longings that unsettle;
I long for the shallow bowls of valleys between
the craggy hills of Wayanad giving a thrill
and seeing things I couldn't imagine
leading into the confines of my brain.

Brooding

I am stressed and distressed to strive
and wrestle and struggle in this weather
in this world of broken relationships
exploitation, rape and murder most foul.
The languages of the heart the cry and sighs
of helplessness and abject negligence
that is rampant in every field and activity
where the poor and needy is sidetracked.
My land seems to be in a grey green light
of a cloudy day reveling in antagonism
and the jumble of inexplicable images
churning chaotically in the heat of my anger.
The omnipresent gloomy shade encapsulates
the sweet blessed memories of childhood
with clouds dense, opaque and hypnotic;
days when even the air filtered down
through the leaves and the constant whooshing
of the rain and wind across the roof
the misty wet that swirled around my head
and the seemingly confusing tragedies

of the world and shifting moods and eyes
still hoping to celebrate this life in this world
seeing with awe the all pervading love
of the creator wishing the heat of my anger
fade into gratitude for this life, the miracle.

A Leap into the Void

A dehumanising dominance
and the all pervading threat of it
experiencing an aloneness, eerie and intense
even the river rippling silently upon the shore
feels a sudden wave of panic movement
creating a frenzy of murderous thoughts.
The rain had been falling all night
full of obscure overtones and subtle shadings
making me wade through my own self;
seeing no great visual treats, but a masked mind
yearning to leap into an empty void.
A mind tired of false trials and wasted times
a weary mind fearing to miss the obvious
and an element of fear in my prejudice
a dread cultivated to evince sympathy
for people who fled to the psychiatrists
trying to cope with the injustices of the world
feeling nothing but a desire for vengeance.
A generation that thirsts for knowledge
flapping the wings of their dreams

going higher and higher forgetting
the ones who gave them the wings..,
and the principles and values often compromised
and forgetting that land with the sweet little brook
and that something visually pleasing yet mysterious
and failing to be responsible for oneself.

Pervading Power

In the fullness of the enchanting silence
I search for the power within that transforms
which I intuitively feel in the flowers that dance
in the breeze that brings the fragrance sweet.
In the rivulets that flow kissing the banks
the vapours that rise upwards from the ocean
in the tears that well up in the eyes of the oppressed
on the faces of the farmers wailing at their crops destroyed
in the eyes of the victims of rape and abuse
in the eyes of the youth deprived of jobs
in the eyes of people struggling to connect.
On a bad day getting worse in the loosing war on crimes
in the intimate moment of recognition and despise
in the beautiful moonlight, though only reflected
in the silence of admiration for sheer brilliance
in the continual struggle to believe in oneself
in life that screws you when you think
you have figured it out and the resulting despair
in times spent in creativity and in climate change,

in the changing colours of autumn season.
And in the creeping weariness brought on
by social pressure and the weary weight of age.

One with Nature

The oneness of the vast canopy of the sky
and the endless horizon of my thoughts
mellowed by age and use, the calm serene voice
the strained silence between prodding gently
a sense of place, a meaning to existence
and a new dimension to work so passionately believed
the citadel that I was hoping to build against
the encroaching tides of my past dreams
using my knowledge to build a better world
where man's inexorable struggle to survive
encountering a stunned self and loneliness
alone with the oneness of nature
and stillness appropriate to the solemn moment
the ecstasy of my private dreams merging
with the awesome grandeur of the world
in a rare moment of silence and introspection
radiating a beauty that I seldom contemplated
and the voice dwindled to an embarrassed mumble.
The mind fled through clear crystal prisms of delight
as the strong concentrated sweetness of Nature

suddenly born over to me on some invisible
movement of air enveloping me as the petals
of the flower enclose and intoxicate the bees
within the world of scent, exquisite ,
penetrating, strong and almost blinding
and I felt dazzled, queer and then very peaceful.

Flicker of Hope

Established order vanishing overnight
a pervading weariness of a possible danger
a wordless humming, tuneless unfathomable
about my own former, now amputated glory.
The amount of unfilled time frightens me
people becoming lethargic and lazy
with eyes uncommunicative and void
faces no more happy and ecstatic
propelled forward by a swollen belly
a mass without words or melody
like the soul of the long suppressed farmer
afraid of the wares of continuous sorrow
like incredibly ancient inscriptions on tomb stones
the pathos of all invisible glory and hope
like the oasis of the forbidden fruit
or like the politician's smile friendly but distant.
Wishing to walk into the invisibility around the corner
I am on a tiny road that leads nowhere
but whatever silenced will clamour to be heard
and darkness shall lift into the sky upon the horizon

and the tension I feel shall evaporate like a subterranean hum
and the air shall be suffused with fragrance of love
at the pleasant view of the rolling countryside.

Wayanadan Farmers

Sitting on my balcony day dreaming
watching the retreating rains leaving
a trail of destruction and suffering;
the unreasonably muddy rainy days
plunging the farmers to another year of want.
Empathising with silent contemplation
of the devastated land and all the dimensions
of the plight of people with their faces
expressionless and void of any emotion
and the lines that crinkled the corners
of their eyes and the deepening furrows
on either side of their noses
and wounded minds refusing to be healed
a perpetual reproach to the Government.
In another time and place, in another life
they may live in fascinated disbelief!!
Being alone and too much to themselves
they sit smelling the turned earth;
from a distance it appears to be peace
knowing there can be no peace without justice.

They were ambitious people with big dreams
caught in a situation of struggle and survival;
let me pass my time in sulky wordlessness
experiencing the ecstasy of abasement.

Unreal Melody

I woke up from a nightmare
to the calm reality and familiar surroundings
the gentle breeze warm as a lover's caress and to a smile,
the universal gesture of peace and goodwill.
The snow capped mountain
too picturesque to be real
watching mist of clouds
covering its highest peaks,
I am a long way from home.
Waiting for the day to come when public
recognise the best person by his accomplishments,
not by the false promises or slander our politicians
seem wont to stand upon for our votes.
I feel like playing a role in an imaginary plot
and search for dreams and dwell in the past
wishing to spend the rest of my life
in complete peace and ease
where no thoughts would plunge into hopeless despair
and my room filled with a pregnant silence
where voices vibrant with excitement whisper

'Love is to behold a vision of perfection',
a panorama of colour and spectacle
and life of quiet dignity and genuine regard
where rulers turn attention to advancements
of life and to its real fulfillment
and stop chanting a strange unreal melody
understanding the depth of personal misery of the poor.

Churning

Sitting beneath the tiered fringes down in the shade
looking at the river gives me a sense
of timelessness; a moment of silence
to get lost in a world within
and think of the complicated pattern of life.
There is ugliness of life everywhere
a stench of death, sickness, rape and despair
no robust, simple stir of life
and no cool sweet smell of flowers
and the common man's future
lies like fallen monuments long forgotten.
I wonder the water is churning or the river safe
or nursing an evil grievance of currents?
Yet the view miles down the river
is one of the most beautiful in the world.
Watching the clouds covering the mountain
and my mind oppressed by the invisible
presence of some long forgotten backdrop
as the sun went down behind the mountain
and the pale river thinned into the horizon

while the intense conflict in the mind prevents
giving feeling visual to the churning within
and my half formed thoughts trailed and merged.

Unsettled Mind

I am left in the cool unquiet alone
in the room, flooded with the morning radiance
and the intense churning within
makes me think I am in the company
of Iphigenia's ghost or wondering
what Orpheus's last song
to Eurydice might have been.
A calm suddenly descending on me
as if I were looking at myself from far away, above.
I try to smile; but the expression disintegrate
into the cloying tendrils of childhood receding.
I become more awake as my little village began to twinkle
though the landscape seemed darker, the colours tarnished
I listen to the traffic and the wind
wondering whether I am drowning in my dreams;
the mood grim to the point of suffocation
keeping any sense of lightness at bay.
Slices of light glowing inside the latched shutters of mind;
there are layers here, thousands of years of life and death

and untold history of escape from violence, hunger, disease, famines

while I try to understand the nebula that is the end.

The aging night gathering her night skirts

as little drops of perspiration blooming along my forehead

feeling suddenly old like drops of water in a pool

making a little wave and then fade away into nothing.

Nostalgia

The first glint of sunrise was a pink halo
over a hill above my village, Payyampally.
It strained through the trees and was turning
to yellow, then to orange; no clouds
nothing but brilliant colours against a dark sky
the fleeting grace of a new season.
My heart swelled until all the loss,
all the grief, the loneliness and self-abasement
of my life washed away by the sky
and a cloud that draped the face
of the moon that looked like a wedding veil
amongst the frozen stars staring at me.
My villagers mystify me, their lowliness
their plain looks, their lack of aspirations
their ignorance of things so vital
their tone plaintive but oddly cheerful
their tears of grief, of anger, of disillusionment,
their life indifferent to the marvels around
with a hard life marked by many losses
with sad twists and turns of fate.

I watch the sky darken and the shadows
engulf the whole world and the clouds
sliding past a lonely pale moon.
I think of all the smiles and waves
sweet oranges and Japanese gardens;
aimless walks, mosquitoes nibbling
on hands and legs and faces blazing with excitements,
of the uncertainties that lurk beneath
the hollow promises of politicians
and as the car moved looking back
to see my students receding, see them
disappear in the clouds of dust and exhaust.
Parents no more, and I am here
in a strange place and people
separated from the life I had known
by the great cooling towers and coalfields
the many factories spitting thick black smoke.
Now all these familiar peoples and things gone
I feel uprooted, displaced like an intruder
on someone else's land, a stranger in my own village.
A tightening chest, a room reeling
up and down, ground shifting beneath my legs
and a forlornness descending like a shroud.

Crisis of Conscience

A deep paralysing grief
that surges within my chest;
a never ending grief
changing colour all the time,
not a sign of weakness,
or a lack of faith
but a price of love.
Our age old tolerance that sustained us
disappearing into the incredible
vortex of communal disharmony
speaking in a conspiratorial whisper.
The malady of dictatorial democracy
released by life dominated by the supernatural.
As for me the day is far spent;
experiencing heat and hate waves mingling.
Hate frenzy, vile speeches, violence communal;
crumbling institutions, police as agents,
rising unemployment, surging inflation;
and hiding myself from myself
fearing to meet my rebuking conscience

fleeing like Cain all the time
asking "am I the keeper of my brother?"
The economy on the edge
while tricks of mass "distraction "
like fear psychosis purposely created
numbs the ability of the common man
to react constructively to injustices
living with doubts and anxiety ever present
and pressed down by the weight of living
sinking deeper into an irrational world.

Conflict Zone

A great tragedy envelops the whole world
a tragedy of blatant display of power and arrogance
of heads of nations, religions and political parties
threatening the very fabric of any kind of order
creating an atmosphere of confusion and chaos.
There is a slow sad close-lipped smile everywhere
a bewildered, hollow-eyed frightening look.
Waves of sorrow swell and crash
then again swell and crash one after another.
Years ago I saw the pain of hunger and famine
in the eyes of the dying children of Eritrea
hair ruffled by the wind eyes crinkled against the sun.
Now I see children, old, disabled thrown out
like a heaving sea tossing the ships in fierce storm
uprooted, displaced, devastated in an invasion so massive
the helpless fleeing their native land
In the midst of death and destruction;
a man made human tragedy so frightening and haunting
and my mind a conflict zone where horror images make
impossible even the wish for some tranquillizing music.

Acute alienation and the depth of darkness ahead

the confused and displaced, a life too much to bear, too far away

while the rumbling of thunder and lightning flickering

from the weapons of destruction continually showering shells

as relationships become victim of arrogance and selfishness

and my wish to find an opportunity to create meaning for life

falls apart in the drift and rift of conflicting emotions.

Riverside Village

Sunlight filtered through the blinds casting neat lines
across my bed

and staring at the eastern sky where a hint of orange was
peeking through scattered clouds; as the sky grew brighter
and clouds dissipated

I was filled with joy absorbing the landscape

and the fascinating views of the Western Ghats;

the exhilarating and magnificent act of nature.

Walking through the tiny town and tribal hamlets

saw my childhood tribal friend staring at me

and a thousand thoughts swirled wildly through my brain

and a ripple of excitement at the sudden meeting.

I hugged him for a long time and when released

he was suddenly hit with emotion struggling to speak;

but words refused to come and my heart ached for him.

Covering my face I fought back the tears.

He grew up in a society so willing to ignore

violence against a despised and a suppressed class

and their struggle with the horror of the deeds of the
upper class

and the whispers and sighs of the tormented children.
Lost in another world his wrinkled eyes stared
blankly at something on the receding horizon
as a heavy silence engulfed us as minutes passed
and I waved my hands and he stood there old
like a statue frozen in time with copper and tin.
The midday sun baked the ground around me
as I looked through the fence to the paddy fields beyond;
the fields vast and run to the horizon in all directions
and crops start and seemed to run for ever
while farmers sweating in the field with dried up dreams
and withered lives rubbing the deep burrows of their foreheads
and layers of tiny wrinkles around their eyes.
Stepping out of the shadow of hopelessness and sorrow
into the blinding midday sun and the suffocating air
I reach the village graveyard where many of my childhood friends sleep
where poetry and scriptures and farewells inscribed in granites
and my eyes moistened with memories at once sad and pleasant.
The hilly countryside pretty and the day beautiful
and the cows grazing in the hillside peacefully.
The sun was falling to the west behind
and I marvel at the beauty of my village, Payyampally.

The mountain and the quaint little village grew dim
and Kabini the east flowing river, valleys, hills and meadows began to fade
and darkness brought an eerie quiet to the village as glow worms danced.

Election Fever

Election fever in the midst of a terrible pandemic;
I see the world in which I live in crumbles
around me and reality submerges me
and feel like a weather-vane buffeted by
a swirling wind of apprehensive flicker of recognition
of the emptiness, the banality, the squalor of most lives.
In the solitude of my soul I see no politics of issues;
only the painfully slow movement of govt. machinery
the relentless endeavours of politicians shamelessly
dividing my people in the name of caste, creed and region.
Tension constricting the throats of the people
like the avenging furies of old chasing victims
and a weary, melancholy gaze on the farmer's faces,
while the candidates playing dice with the voters;
the enormity of the destruction of the secular fabric
of this great land of ours and the destiny of its people.
Silence of pain and anguish stills my mind
and wishing nothing would disturb the tranquil pattern

of our existence where tears and laughter inexplicably mingled.

Looking at the dark unfathomable eyes riveted

to some distant vision whose outlines only the poor can perceive

and longing in vain for cold reason to dawn on politicians

and hoping the day would come when like mothers consoling

a weeping child, the politicians would be empathetic to issues

and the chaos and confusion that stifle the emotions of the people.

The character assassination and mud slinging

the politicians not seeing people with thin hands

and faces weathered into a tracery of wrinkles

the furrowed brows waiting for their rightful due.

I look at them with no emotion, no feeling of sorrow or anger

only wishing these people find hope, tangible, palpable hope

as the rain water flickered in the reflected light

of a distant bulb.

Mind

In a chilly little house in Wayanad
in the north east of the State of Kerala
probing the mysteries of human mind
hoping the seeds of clemency will grow
in the garden of our minds so fertile
where all beings are intimately connected
to the Universal Energy as an integral part.
There are dreams and scenery and desires
that inspire and imagination that transpires
coexisting so peacefully under the same roof.
At times many ambitions without vision
to fill the moral responsibility to society
though enmeshed, still with the power
to drill through time and distance giving
constructive responses to broken lives
it offers a stunning study in disorganization.
The bridge providing a splendid view of Kabini
flowing so gracefully to the holy river Cauvery
unlike my chaotic and perturbed mind never
mixing or mingling with the universal mind.

The mind oftentimes like a dungeon, dark and cold
water dripping from above with many dark
secrets and many voices moving high and low
with the dramatic flair of a fine actor;
and like a strange little corner of the world
life the indefinable phantom in a garden fine
not growing gracefully or peacefully old.
Getting out of this dark and complex world
longing for the long walks by the ocean shore
watching the sun sink slowly into the ocean
veiling the forlorn history of this moody world;
listening with fascination to the stories of the waves
as my face getting more worried and wrinkled
and life at times a nasty secret, dark and deep.

Existential Crisis

One more year closer to the final fight
growing old with the worldly temptations
failing to abnegate self and its conflicts
faltering with all the flaws and foibles
playing a series of discordant notes
the journey of life struts seeking the shore
or lighthouse to port to anchor downing sail
and overcome all the existential crisis.
Before me long secluded expanses
of endless forests with many voices,
each voice a thread weaving such
a sorrowful melody in the wilderness
of my chest like a bird trapped behind
a glass door wanting to dance like
butterflies in the cool breeze outside.
Heard a holy jubilation, a swell
of cheers from the passing clouds
and I stumbled into a merciful sleep
under naked branches and whispering stars
and that moment I ripped out the seams

of my own dreams and patched them into theirs.
Their laughter seemed less spontaneous
more like a performance for an audience
orchestrated for public consumption.
The gasping and whooping sound of sirens
mingle with the risk and triumphs, the misery
and the rain of tears of the families of the dying
pouring down on the uncreated conscience of my race.
I try to make sense of my own existence
trying to grow from bearing witness
to the importance of human relationships
in the midst of pandemic and hardships
asking if the weight of mortality does not grow
does it at least get more familiar with age ?

Change

I wasn't certain that was progress
but it sure as hell was change
I mourn for the dear departed days
when all of Payyampally was a cow pasture.
I allow myself a small pang of nostalgia
remembering my boyhood and vacations
an air of modest prosperity.
A home that was warm and clean
happy family with love enough
to go round and more to share
a mouth full of strong white teeth.
I search for God in the people;
will you be there to close my eyes?
What I think mine is to be sacrificed
the sacrifice must happen in the mind.
The frightening silence, the mournful
atmosphere of sighs that speak;
justice of God that forgives,
justice that forgets and gives hope.
Challenges excites me not confining;

soft philosophical musings
in victory there is failure
time will devour all victories.

Dalits

After spending the best part of my life
with the Dalits and the less privileged
and hearing oftentimes thundering calls
for the untouchables to shake off
the undermining slavish mentality
and claim their long denied political power
and push back against the feelings
of failure and quit the self pity
and take charge of their own destiny,
they are where they have been for ages.
Betrayed by politicians for their gains
and kept divided by the powers that be
their life never moving in an orderly pace
finding it difficult to keep their family happy
their faces betraying emotions save pride
they are unaware of their own disadvantages.
The quiet cruel, nuances of not belonging
like a cork floating on the ocean of another place
the natives displaced by the intruders
and told there are other ways of being

and feel more distant like a place in imagination
never allowed to be under one umbrella.
At times I have felt their shouts puncturing
the silence with cheerful shouts
and felt the warm tug of the past
something deeper than what I normally feel
the slow shift of generational gears;
painful but time pushes us all forward.
I still love reading lofty works of literature and philosophy
and am convinced strong policies and will
and governmental action is needed
for any meaningful social change.
I speak wistfully of friends and family
have spent hours listening to people
describe their challenges and aspirations
enduring misery for the sake of convictions
wanting to be sincere far more than being rich.
Build trust in your strength which is lacking
fight cynicism bred from disappointments
from a thousand small failures over time
amid the fears and frustrations and absences
and disenfranchisement and helplessness
and shoot an arrow in the opposite direction.

Baffling

A wave of dizziness and nausea baffled my brain
while the bright sunlight bathed my little village
the vagrant scattered thoughts
and I wished I could lay still and be.
I see a jay looking at me through the branches
of the tree and I smiled at it with numb pleasure
marveling at the symmetry of wings and form
yet unable to find words to express
adequately what I was feeling.
The feel of cool, dewy grass on my hands
I long to be completely at peace with the world
but a horror reaching into my heart squeezing
pressing me to put prudence ahead of daring.
The bright mid morning turning into a dusky afternoon
as the immensity of the task ahead staggers me
no fire or brimstone but a bone wrenching
weariness that weighed so heavily upon
the heart that felt ready to burst under the strain.
The weakness behind my knees
ask for the comfort I so terribly wanted

yet this isn't the time for displays of weakness.
The pale sun dropping below the tops of the trees
spoke with the conviction of someone
finally face to face with the reality
of what my beliefs so convincingly implied,
I see the sun inching closer to the horizon
and feel a shiver race up my spine
like a knife being traced along my vertebrae.
Words that lingered beyond understanding
and a wave of hideous shrieking laughter
erupted around me deafening in its intensity.
An unholy congregation moving with silence
and a solid wall of panic slammed into my mind
bothering the uncertainty of what lay on the path
paralysing the vibrant power within me
like a wisp of smoke in a brisk wind,
it is gone and seemed so far away
like fragments from another life or world.

Dreams

A slow reversal of situation sets in
and a new airiness to my thoughts
and happy with my freedom, happy with others
happy the way the world is moving
the leaping and charging the rippling and roaring
my feelings too deep or too jumbled to share.
The advent of spring fails to warm up the air
feeling of fear and flight, the travails of life,
with able bodied people denied access to their due
causing resentment and mistrust and live
with the bitter residue of their dashed dreams.
Here the rules of survival are very different
what is happening is unjust but so common;
a people failing in the mercy they preach
while the dictators take away our freedom to choose
with so many exceptions to so many rules.
Standing at the crossroads of the old and young
no one here seems responsible and no one to blame
with limited resources and time I am pushed into silence
and nothing capable of filling the void within

I struggle in vain to keep saving for a rainy day.

The world of high drama and intrigue

the tyranny of shifting hierarchies and alliances

the youth being raised in the cross currents of the great flux

my own courage to advocate for myself fails

this country and its people and I become numb

and yet accepting what comes and move forward

hoping for new temperaments, new dreams

and a new generation with spirits deep and strong.

End

Pain lanced into every organ hammering
at my heart, my lungs, my head
the dizzy, dark silence that followed,
I sensed my fate was being debated
with cold, remorseless logic
where once there had been pain,
there was now only a distant throbbing
a numbness that reached down through
my cheeks and settled in over my head
like a blanket of snow on a peak.
A gesture of friendship that I hoped
would penetrate the wall of trauma,
the nothingness that surrounded me
was absolute, final and irreversible.
After all the years, after all the waiting
I finally made it back; after all the years
of grief and struggle, the silence
of the cemetery was almost anticlimactic.
Strange, I thought, in this place of death
to feel that I had finally come home

where the spirits of night, the dark allies
that lurked deep in the earth rallies;
the fight fierce and so terrible,
full of fury, blood and frightening,
my own world graveyard then plummeted
to the ground like a rock falling from a peak.

Peace and Tranquility

The sea is calm like a child sleeping
on its mother's lap and the full moon
smiles on the world below while
the high tides of pride and selfishness
causing the river of compassion and empathy
wind it's way through the mountain of egos
vanishing into the depth of ignorance and avarice
annihilating the waves of goodwill in men.
Sitting beneath the dying shades of woods
looking at the mountain of Egos cold and forbidding
watching the humanitarian crisis of a warring world
and drying up of the milk of human kindnesses
where every one busy amalgamating power
by annexing neighbours and territories
a blind craving for the fleeting worldly possessions
leading to sex, drugs, violence and loss of values.
I see the beacon light from the lighthouse
inviting the world to a conversion of mind and manners
leading to a reversal of situation and relationships
creating a sober caring and sharing humankind

caressed by the waves of tranquility and peace
emanating from unconditional forgiveness
leading mankind to amazingly new pastures
and thick woodlands perennially watered.

A Conceptual Crisis

Amazed at the information they possess
and appalled by the sight of suicides by youngsters;
a tragedy so intense, complex, bewildering
a dilemma needing urgent solution
and a constructive concern for persons
who in the dark recesses of human mind
where the unheard sighs and suppressed tears
playing havoc and creating a Maya effect
pushing them to run away from life.
A curiosity to know causes of things and beyond
see a generation of parents and teachers
with an obsession to create little Pygmalions
pressurising children mercilessly to perform
pushing to the brink and forcing them
to withdraw to a shimmering crystal globe
becoming lonelier than ever in the face of challenges
and unhealthy competitions leading to
heartbreaks and internal conflicts so intense.
Children reduced to mere passive receptacles
receiving information from teachers and books;

never empowering them to become individual
and creators of their own world and dreams
creating a crisis of learning in the children.
Failing to offer the comfort of physical presence
or intervene at the right time in the right way
concerned only with the physical well-being
the enigma of human behaviour remaining hidden.
Sexual violations and domestic violence
a busy world not having time to the silent sighs
a guilty conscience like cancer devastating life
and the lack of a properly appreciative relationship
helping suicidal and homicidal tendencies to develop.
A mystery defiled rational explication
a state of disorientation and isolation
suddenly sad, sits in silence, with vacant eyes.
Human behaviour endlessly different
life becoming so disordered and chaotic
trying to make sense out of the senseless
or logic, the sequence or connecting link
finally a desperate step and a frustrated leap
and the sighs of the bereaved, a great wall of silence.

Lost Chance

She stood on the other side of the stream
with an agoraphobic look at the river in spate
her dark thick hair splaying about
her shoulders in a silken skein
and a bewildering gesture of movement.
Her chiseled features giving her a whimsical charm;
but the sweet innocence in her expression
suddenly turned into murderous frenzy,
as she saw the dark menacing clouds gathering
and her bleary eyes no longer glistening
as the day turned miserable with lowering clouds.
Sharp gusts of rain and mean menacing wind
coming out whipping even the desire to live .
My thought process becoming more chaotic
bewilderment and disorientations and afraid
of being swept away by disorder, anger and anguish,
at our self-centred leaders never learning
though Nature continually teaches the world
that climate change is as real as price rise.
I look across the river to see her once again;

but alas! the river ravaged by the fury
of torrential unseasonal rains swallowed her and my fantasies
leaving me with a sympathy for the lost chances
to search for God in people in need
as the dark day began to fade into darkness.

A Leap into the Void

A dehumanising dominance
and the all pervading threat of it
experiencing an aloneness, eerie and intense
even the river rippling silently upon the shore
feels a sudden wave of panic movement
creating a frenzy of murderous thoughts.
The rain had been falling all night
full of obscure overtones and subtle shadings
making me wade through my own self;
seeing no great visual treats, but a masked mind
yearning to leap into an empty void.
A mind tired of false trials and wasted times
a weary mind fearing to miss the obvious
and an element of fear in my prejudice
a dread cultivated to evince sympathy
for people who fled to the psychiatrists
trying to cope with the injustices of the world
feeling nothing but a desire for vengeance.
A generation that thirsts for knowledge
flapping the wings of their dreams

going higher and higher forgetting
the ones who gave them the wings..,
and the principles and values often compromised
and forgetting that land with the sweet little brook
and that something visually pleasing yet mysterious
and failing to be responsible for oneself.

Death

There are seasons and regenerations
the soil seems to come alive
with grubs and bugs and worms;
birds chirrup and buds swell
and each part of nature burgeons
at its own pace after winters death.
Will I face the last battle of life with death
with tears of regret silently streaming
down the cheeks for the lost part of life
or bravely engage and grapple like
Jacob with the angel compelling him
to bless till this journey is through,
and thank the Giver of life for its gifts
and crush the waves of death
till the breeze turn warm at the end of Winter
and pass the last few days like dreams
ushering harmony and convergence
of illusion and reality in annihilation?
Or feel like a sob welling up my chest
concealing it with a cough into a kerchief

and left alive but incapable of joy or sorrow
in an air filled with heat and dust
withered and paralysed slipping into oblivion
signaling a violent morning about to dawn
and a judgment where mercy reigns over justice?

Refuge

Families are scattered, hearts broken
waves of pain surging one after another;
and the dark days of terror returns
and the fear drains the beauty of life
as the fabric of a peaceful society
destroyed by a few fundamentalists
and my vision collapsing into
a vacuum of disappointment.
Awaiting a time when I can go
without any checks to where I will
and the freedom to sing like birds
sans any religion, caste or politics
and open the windows of ages
filling my mind with the wisdom of the sages
enabling to read my mind so complex
and give expression to words unspoken for so long.
Playing a delicious melody that scented the wind
under the quivering stillness of the watching trees
as the night shifts her horizon
contemplating the kindling of the dawn

and the damp chill that had settled into night
leading me to Mother Nature's lap
to find meaning of pain, beauty, damnation,
horror and find redemption on her lap
as she sings of a tale of lifelong quest for love.

Shadows and Ripples

Far away in a strange alien land
far away from my native Wayanad
where the Kabini flows whispering the struggle and triumph
of the migrant hardworking men and women
and their shared helplessness, agony and ecstasy
where I used to dream of an alternate reality.
As evening drifted into the realm of weariness
and my eyes roll back into darkness
weary through the ether of time
fractured with shadows and ripples
and the wind rustling the leaves on the branches
like flirting with annihilation.
I look at myself and the natural decay of aging
and the cycle of seasons like the traffic light
changing from red to green and yellow again
and then again rhythmically unreeling;
then evoking the lost world of childhood
I plod and ponder and at times persist
seeing the looming shadow of swift decline.

I hear the frightened eerie gasping voices
the helpless lakhs and the monster Corona
our Shiva the destroyer of human vanity.
My mind the labyrinth of time
where people and places come and go
like fleeting series of images
asking are we to be vanquished
defeated by forces unknown??
The time would come sooner
when I would unlikely have the stamina
or the time to say "Thank You" for loving me.
Andrew, my little grandson curls up beside
bringing me back to time and reality
and once again I dream not of the past
but of the wide-open future for him.

www.ingramcontent.com/pod-product-compliance
Lightning Source LLC
LaVergne TN
LVHW061555070526
838199LV00077B/7055